Why Do We Need Water?

Kelley MacAulay

Crabtree Publishing Company
www.crabtreebooks.com

Author
Kelley MacAulay

Publishing plan research and development
Reagan Miller

Notes to adults
Reagan Miller

Editor
Crystal Sikkens

Proofreader
Adrianna Morganelli

Design
Tammy McGarr

Photo research
Tammy McGarr, Crystal Sikkens

**Production coordinator
and prepress technician**
Tammy McGarr

Print coordinator
Margaret Amy Salter

Illustrations
Barbara Bedell: page 24

Photographs
Thinkstock: pages 22, 24 (reusing)
All other images by Shutterstock

Library and Archives Canada Cataloguing in Publication

MacAulay, Kelley, author
        Why do we need water / Kelley MacAulay.

(Natural resources close-up)
Includes index.
Issued in print and electronic formats.
ISBN 978-0-7787-0494-2 (bound).--ISBN 978-0-7787-0498-0 (pbk.).--
ISBN 978-1-4271-8219-7 (html).--ISBN 978-1-4271-8223-4 (pdf)

        1. Water-supply--Juvenile literature. 2. Water use--Juvenile
literature. I. Title.

GB662.3.M23 2014   j553.7   C2014-900384-6
                                                     C2014-900385-4

Library of Congress Cataloging-in-Publication Data

MacAulay, Kelley.
        Why do we need water? / Kelley MacAulay.
            pages cm. -- (Natural resources close-up)
        Includes index.
        ISBN 978-0-7787-0494-2 (reinforced library binding : alk. paper) -- ISBN 978-0-
7787-0498-0 (pbk. : alk. paper) -- ISBN 978-1-4271-8219-7 (electronic html : alk.
paper) -- ISBN 978-1-4271-8223-4 (electronic pdf : alk. paper)
        1. Water--Juvenile literature. 2. Water conservation--Juvenile literature. I. Title.

        GB662.3.M26 2014
        333.91--dc23

                                              2014002291

Crabtree Publishing Company

www.crabtreebooks.com   1-800-387-7650

Printed in the USA/052014/SN20140313

Published in Canada
Crabtree Publishing
616 Welland Ave.
St. Catharines, Ontario
L2M 5V6

Published in the United States
Crabtree Publishing
PMB 59051
350 Fifth Avenue, 59th Floor
New York, New York 10118

Published in the United Kingdom
Crabtree Publishing
Maritime House
Basin Road North, Hove
BN41 1WR

Published in Australia
Crabtree Publishing
3 Charles Street
Coburg North
VIC 3058

Contents

Blue planet 4

Gifts from nature . . .6

Salt water. 8

Fresh water. 10

Living under water . .12

Living near water . . .14

So many uses 16

Sharing water 18

Keep water clean. . .20

Reusing water 22

Words to know 24

Blue planet

Look at this picture of Earth. The blue color you see is water. Water covers more than 70% of Earth's surface!

Water is all around us. It pours from your tap. It may run in a stream near your home. It falls from the sky as rain. Water is very important. There would be no life on Earth without water.

Gifts from nature

Living things need water to survive. People and animals drink water every day. Plants take in water to grow.

What do you think?

Plants are natural resources. How are they used?

Water is a natural resource.

Natural resources are things from nature that people use. Take a deep breath. The air you breathe is a natural resource.

Salt water

There are two types of water. One type of water is **salt water**. Salt water has salt in it. People and animals cannot drink salt water. Almost all the water on Earth is salt water.

salt

Most salt water is in oceans. Oceans are huge areas of water. They are very deep. Large ships can travel on oceans. They carry people or items to different places.

Fresh water

The other type of water is **fresh water**. Fresh water does not have salt in it. People and animals drink fresh water. Lakes and rivers have fresh water.

What do you think?

How is the water in oceans different than the water in lakes?

ice

Most fresh water on Earth is frozen as ice.

It cannot be used by people or animals.

Ice is found in the coldest places on Earth.

Living under water

Many animals live under water. Huge whales live in deep oceans. Shiny salmon race through rivers. Thousands of colorful fish find homes in **coral reefs**. Coral reefs are rocky areas in warm oceans.

People breathe air using body parts called **lungs**. You must hold your breath when you go under water. Fish can breathe under water using body parts called **gills**. Gills allow fish to take in air from the water.

Living near water

Most living things find homes in places where there is fresh water. Animals drink water from lakes, rivers, and rain puddles. Plants take in water from the ground through their **roots**. Roots are plant parts that are underground.

roots

rain forest

desert

It rains every day in rain forests. They are crowded with plant and animal life. Deserts get little rain. Fewer plants and animals live there.

So many uses

Think about how many times a day you use water. You drink water. You clean yourself with it. You use water to brush your teeth. Your clothes are washed in water.

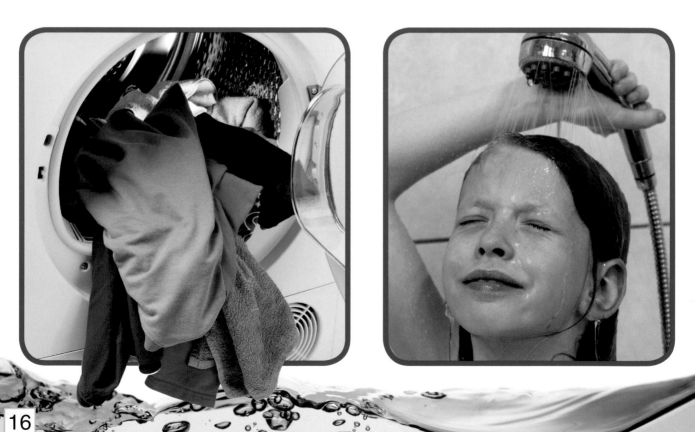

In some places people do not have water in their homes. They must carry water to their homes. They only have a little water to use, so they have to use it carefully.

Sharing water

Animals need clean water, too. They drink water and find food in it. Animals also use water to bathe, or clean themselves.

The water on Earth must be shared by all living things. It is important not to waste water. Turn off taps tightly so they do not drip. Take a quick shower rather than a bath.

What do you think?

This boy has turned off the taps while brushing his teeth. How does this action save water?

Keep water clean

All living things need clean water. Garbage on the ground or chemicals that have been poured down the drain can end up in water. This makes water unclean. Drinking unclean water makes people sick. Animals cannot live in unclean water.

What do you think?

How can you stop garbage from getting into water?

Reusing water

We must take care of Earth's natural resources. Saving and **reusing** resources is important. To reuse something means to use it again. Reusing things creates less waste. You can use clean bath water to wash your car!

What do you think?

Gardens are beautiful, but they need a lot of water. This girl is watering the garden with rain water. How can you save rain water to water plants when it is dry?

Words to know

 **coral reefs** 12

 **fresh water** 10, 11, 14

 **gills** 13

lungs 13

reusing 22

roots 14

salt water 8, 9

Notes to adults and an activity

Discuss before activity
How do living things use water?
Why is it important to take care of Earth's water?

Activity: Children experience how difficult it is to filter water after a disaster, such as an oil spill.
Materials: container, vegetable or olive oil, strainer, coffee filters, paper towel, newspaper, cotton balls
Directions
1. Pour water into plastic container. Add enough oil to create a layer on top of water.
2. Explain to readers that the oil pollutes the water. Their goal is to use the materials given to remove the pollution from the water.
3. Give children time to discuss how they can use the materials to remove pollution.
4. Have children use each of the materials to filter the water. Encourage children to record their results and identify which materials work best.
5. As a group, discuss the results of their experiment. Were children able to remove all pollution from the water? Use responses to reinforce the importance of keeping water free from pollution.

Learning More

Books
Living things need water by Bobbie Kalman. Crabtree Publishing Company, 2007.

Save Water by Kay Barnham. Crabtree Publishing Company, 2007.

Sources of water by Rebecca Olien. Capstone Publishing Company, 2005.

Websites
This site promotes water stewardship, with links to educational games that reinforce water conservation.
www.miwaterstewardship.org/youthstewards/online-watergames

This website has many kid-friendly links to water-related games, conservation activities, and projects.
http://wateruseitwisely.com/kids/